The Kent State Massacre: The History and Legacy of the Shootings That Shocked America

By Charles River Editors

A student jumps in a pool of blood on the ground after the shootings

About Charles River Editors

Charles River Editors provides superior editing and original writing services across the digital publishing industry, with the expertise to create digital content for publishers across a vast range of subject matter. In addition to providing original digital content for third party publishers, we also republish civilization's greatest literary works, bringing them to new generations of readers via ebooks.

Sign up here to receive updates about free books as we publish them, and visit Our Kindle Author Page to browse today's free promotions and our most recently published Kindle titles.

Introduction

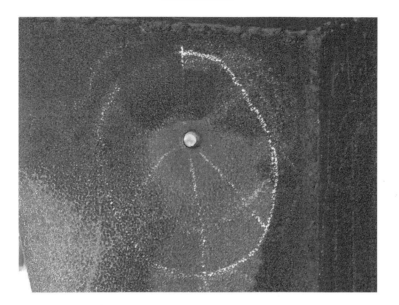

A bullet hole in the Solar Totem #1 sculpture on the Kent St. campus

The Kent State Massacre (May 4, 1970)

"Suddenly, they turned around, got on their knees, as if they were ordered to, they did it all together, aimed. And personally, I was standing there saying, they're not going to shoot, they can't do that. If they are going to shoot, it's going to be blank." – One eyewitness to the shootings

The Vietnam War was one of the most controversial events in American history, and political arguments over the war brought about massive cultural changes across the country during the 1960s. The war ultimately fueled the hippie counterculture, and anti-war protests spread across the country on campuses and in the streets. While some protesters spread peace and love, others rioted, and in August 1968, riots broke out in the streets of Chicago, leading to incredible scenes of National Guardsmen and police confronting 10,000 anti-war rioters during the Democratic National Convention.

By the end of the decade, Vietnam had left tens of thousands of Americans dead, spawned a counterculture with millions of protesters, and destroyed a presidency, but there was plenty more yet to come. Vietnam was already wildly unpopular by 1970, but when President Nixon announced the bombing of Cambodia on April 30, 1970, protests exploded across college campuses. Some of those protests took place at Kent State in Kent, Ohio, and the state's governor replied by declaring a state of emergency and sending the Ohio National Guard to the campus.

On May 4, a Monday, thousands of Kent State students decided to attend protests instead of class. Jeff Miller and his friends had tear gas shot at them by the Ohio National Guard, and Miller picked up one of the tear gas canisters and threw it back at the Guardsmen. At 12:24 p.m., some of the Guardsmen opened fire with live rounds. Miller was instantly killed by a shot through the mouth, and three others lay dead. None of the people wounded or killed were within 70 feet of the Guardsmen, and in the commotion of the scene, photographer John Filo took a picture of Miller's body, surrounded by confused bystanders and a kneeling girl holding up her hands as if to ask, "Why?" The photo would win the Pulitzer Prize that year.

The shootings of unarmed protesters rattled the nation and inevitably led to hardened feelings and further protests. In the aftermath, other college student protesters hung banners that read "They Can't Kill Us All," and hundreds of campuses were brought to a standstill by protesting. Later estimates concluded that 4 million students joined protests across the country, and a protest in Washington, D.C. attracted about 100,000 in the days following the shootings. While both supporters and opponents of the war continued to debate with each other, sometimes heatedly, the shootings at Kent State led to Nixon's establishment of the President's Commission on Campus Unrest, and that group's report went on to claim, "Even if the guardsmen faced danger, it was not a danger that called for lethal force. The 61 shots by 28 guardsmen certainly cannot be justified. Apparently, no order to fire was given, and there was inadequate fire control discipline on Blanket Hill. The Kent State tragedy must mark the last time that, as a matter of course, loaded rifles are issued to guardsmen confronting student demonstrators."

The Kent State Shootings chronicles the events that led up to one of the country's most notorious campus shootings, and the watershed moment that it came to represent for America during the Vietnam War. Along with pictures of important people, places, and events, you will learn about the Kent State shootings like never before, in no time at all.

The Kent State Massacre: The History and Legacy of the Shootings That Shocked America

About Charles River Editors

Introduction

Chapter 1: Tin Soldiers and Nixon's Comin'

"We have been too often disappointed by the optimism of the American leaders, both in Vietnam and Washington, to have faith any longer in the silver linings they find in the darkest clouds…For it seems now more certain than ever that the bloody experience of Vietnam is to end in a stalemate…To say that we are closer to victory today is to believe, in the face of the evidence, the optimists who have been wrong in the past. To suggest we are on the edge of defeat is to yield to unreasonable pessimism. To say that we are mired in stalemate seems the only realistic, yet unsatisfactory, conclusion…it is increasingly clear to this reporter that the only rational way out then will be to negotiate, not as victors, but as an honorable people who lived up to their pledge to defend democracy, and did the best they could." - Walter Cronkite

War has never been popular in America, even as it's widely forgotten that people protested against the colonists during the Revolution and some burned James Madison in effigy during the War of 1812. So many people opposed the way Lincoln was handling the Civil War that he was in danger of losing his bid for reelection in 1864. Naturally, the opposition was even more pronounced once America began to fight wars overseas, with many opposing American involvement in the World Wars until Americans were targeted themselves.

However, the most famous anti-war protests in American history came during the Vietnam War, and it shocked many just how ingrained the protests became in American culture. During President Kennedy's administration, a seemingly small crisis began to grow as the French, on the verge of losing the Southeast Asian colony of French Indochina to communist rebels supported by China and the Soviet Union, separated the colony into two parts: North Vietnam, which would be a pro-communist state, and South Vietnam, which was aligned with the West. However, South Vietnam quickly became embroiled in its own guerrilla war against communist insurgents who wanted to unify it with North Vietnam, and President Kennedy, following President Truman's containment policy, offered limited aid to South Vietnam to prevent it from falling into communist hands.

After President Kennedy's assassination, President Johnson realized that direct U.S. military assistance was needed to prevent South Vietnam from falling to communists. He ordered U.S. navy ships to the area. On August 2, 1964, the USS Maddox was patrolling in the Gulf of Tonkin when it was fired upon by North Vietnamese torpedo boats. Though no Americans were hurt, naval crews were on heightened alert. Two days later, the *Maddox* and USS *Turner Joy* were certain they were being followed by hostile North Vietnamese boats, and both fired at targets popping up on their radar.

After that second "encounter," now known as the Gulf of Tonkin Incident, President Johnson approved air strikes against the North Vietnamese, and Congress approved military action with the Gulf of Tonkin Resolution. By the end of the year, over 16,000 Americans were stationed in South Vietnam. It would be years before the government revealed that the second encounter was no encounter at all. The government never figured out what the Maddox and Turner Joy were firing at that night, but there was no indication that it involved the North Vietnamese.

After the Gulf of Tonkin, President Johnson ordered air strikes against North Vietnam. For the next several years, North Vietnam was the most bombed place on the planet. American bombers dropped tons and tons of bombs on the "Ho Chi Minh Trail," but the Viet Cong kept coming. Johnson had sent fewer than 5,000 Marines to Vietnam in early 1965, but he quickly upped it to 200,000 by the end of the year. There was no going back.

The United States military was poorly suited to the counterinsurgency role it had in South Vietnam, as it had been built to fight conventional battles against Soviet-aligned forces as it had done in the Korean War. Vietnamese communists for the most part did not seek conventional battles with U.S. forces, and when they did, they lost. However, Vietnamese communist forces were able to cause significant casualties against American and South Vietnamese forces and use guerrilla techniques to undermine the South Vietnamese government.

Although hundreds of thousands protested the war in 1967, including Martin Luther King, Jr., a majority of the public still supported it, due in large part to the Johnson's administration public confidence. But as General Westmoreland talked of victory at the end of 1967, the Viet Cong launched a massive assault across South Vietnam in January 1968. Known as the Tet Offensive, the Viet Cong suffered hundreds of thousands of casualties, and the American forces never lost a battle. But American support for the war still plummeted.

As American casualties mounted, the anti-war movement in the United States built, eventually forcing President Johnson to not run for reelection in 1968. However, the splintering of the Democratic Party, as well as the assassination of Robert F. Kennedy, helped Republican Richard Nixon win a tightly contested election that November. Nixon won in part by promising American voters that he had a plan to extricate America from the mess that had become the Vietnam War, but he didn't go in specifics.

Nixon

By 1968, not only were the protests themselves well established, but the attitudes of most campus leadership were likewise set in stone. Peter Jedick, a student at Kent State at the time of the shootings, later explained, "I met with, one of the first things was I met with, I think his name was Dean [Murvin] Perry, at Taylor Hall, which was the journalism school…While I was talking to him, he had a nice window over the commons, and there was a protest going on. There were maybe ten people out there. And I was kind of stupid, because things were going on in California, I guess, and maybe New York, but we were in the middle of the country, we were always three or four years behind everybody else. I said, 'What's going on out there?' He said, 'Oh, they're a bunch of Communists, don't even pay attention to them.' I hate to say this about Mr. Perry, because…I heard he was a great dean, but this was the attitude at the time…So this was like a small, a little group of people protesting, and not even enough to even pay attention to when I first came here."

Nixon would go on to become one of the most maligned Americans in history as a result of Watergate, and it turned out that he was poorly equipped to handle the chaos into which the country was descending. Nixon was a politician, not a statesman, and just a few days before the shooting at Kent State, he told the country:

> "My fellow Americans, we live in an age of anarchy, both abroad and at home. We see mindless attacks on all the great institutions which have been created by free civilizations in the last 500 years. Even here in the United States, great universities are being systematically destroyed.... If, when the chips are down, the world's most powerful nation, the United States of America, acts like a pitiful, helpless giant, the forces of totalitarianism and anarchy will threaten free nations and free institutions throughout the world. It is not our power but our will and character that is being tested tonight...I have rejected all political considerations in making this decision...
>
> Whether my party gains in November is nothing compared to the lives of 400,000 brave Americans fighting for our country and for the cause of peace and freedom in Vietnam. Whether I may be a one-term President is insignificant compared to whether by our failure to act in this crisis the United States proves itself to be unworthy to lead the forces of freedom in this critical period in world history. I would rather be a one-term President and do what I believe is right than to be a two-term President at the cost of seeing America become a second rate power and to see this Nation accept the first defeat in its proud 190-year history..."

As Nixon's actions and comments suggested, far from having a plan in place to remove American soldiers from Vietnam, he fully intended to fight on to victory. In fact, it would be a controversial escalation of the fighting that would bring about the anti-war protests on Kent State and the notorious events of May 4, 1970.

Chapter 2: We're Finally on Our Own

"It became a little scarier for me when the streets were blocked off and I remember distinctly an elderly couple in their cars trapped -- the light had turned red, they were stopped in the traffic and they were surrounded by students. And students started to rock the car. And they were scared. They would lock the doors, they rolled up the windows and I think people were just kind of feeling their oats basically. I didn't understand it as being a political sort of an issue. Although some people did mention Vietnam and we were aware that Cambodia had been bombed. And that things had begun down in Ohio State. But, from my perspective it was drinkin' beer, lookin' for guys. I mean that was what it was about. Then it went from there." – Carol Mirman, a student at Kent State in 1970

The wheels for the protest that ended so tragically on the campus of Kent State were set in motion on Thursday evening, April 30, 1970. In the same broadcast quoted above, President Nixon announced that he would be sending American troops into Cambodia, Vietnam's nearest neighbor. He explained his decision:

"Cambodia, a small country of 7 million people, has been a neutral nation since the Geneva agreement of 1954 an agreement, incidentally, which was signed by the Government of North Vietnam.

American policy since then has been to scrupulously respect the neutrality of the Cambodian people…North Vietnam, however, has not respected that neutrality…Tonight, American and South Vietnamese units will attack the headquarters for the entire Communist military operation in South Vietnam. … This is not an invasion of Cambodia. The areas in which these attacks will be launched are completely occupied and controlled by North Vietnamese forces. Our purpose is not to occupy the areas. Once enemy forces are driven out of these sanctuaries and once their military supplies are destroyed, we will withdraw..."

However, in spite of his assurances, many opponents of the war, particularly those on campuses around the country, were not convinced and viewed the bombing of Cambodia as an attempt on Nixon's part to expand the war in Vietnam. Before the broadcast was even over, student groups began meeting and organizing for protests against the government in general and Nixon in particular. Chuck Ayers, a student at Kent State, has since argued that the announcement changed the feeling of the entire campus: "My girlfriend Karen [and I] …were going to go to a film festival that Thursday night in University Auditorium. …somebody walking onto the stage, setting down a little black-and-white portable TV--you know, we're there for a film festival--setting down this little black-and-white portable TV, plugging it in, turning it on, and there was Nixon making the announcement about the invasion of Cambodia. … I think we left early, because it just wasn't much fun after that. …we walked past the ROTC Building. … But as we walked past the building, Karen and I both in mid-step stopped and looked at each other. And I can remember saying, 'You felt that too, huh?' And she said, 'Yeah.' And it was just this strange cold feeling that wasn't like a physical cold. I've just never forgotten that."

The following morning, on Friday, May 1, the first protest began when about 500 students met in the traditional space use for protesting. The Commons was a large, open area conducive to casual gathering by large groups, and in the center of the area was the Victory Bell, a popular symbol on campus for a number of reasons. Among those present that day were a group of history students who took it upon themselves to symbolically bury a copy of the United States Constitution, claiming President Nixon had killed it by sending troops into Cambodia without Congressional approval.

Later in the afternoon, the Black United Students held their own rally, one that had actually been scheduled even before the president announced the bombing of Cambodia, but it was this second rally that caused particular concern among law enforcement. As student activist Timothy Moore explained, "I was very involved with Black United Students from the first day I stepped onto this campus. Black United Students had what I would call revolutionary-minded leadership at that point, where 'Off the pigs' was a common saying because of the violence that they witnessed still happening to black people. So, that violent dimension, and black militants being associated with it, and 'black nationalism' being another term that was mouthed very much during those years. All of those, and, 'Black Power,' of course, which was one of these vague terms that nobody really knew what it meant. But it was something that rallied us just because it sounded so good and had so much power to it."

Jon Ridinger's pictures of The Commons and the Victory Bell

During the rally that Friday afternoon, the students passed around word that there would be another rally the following Monday at noon. Friday evening, as the students spread off campus and out into the community, they gathered at a number of popular hangouts along North Water Street in Kent, Ohio, and as people got drunker, their protests became louder. John Carson, who owned a pharmacy in the area, later recalled, "I was driving in East Main Street, into the downtown area, and suddenly I was in the middle of a crowd. And that's when the, evidently, the sheriff had been called in by that then mayor, and I was driving a brand new Buick convertible, and they were saying 'Kill the mayor,' and I'm thinking, I hope they know who the mayor is. And I wasn't sure who these guys with the shotguns were, because the sheriff came out of uniform. … And the crowd got unruly by this point, they were throwing a lot of stones and things, and there were some breakage. … There were some motorcyclists in town, and there were a few guys up on boxes--orange crates as we used to say--speaking out against the war and so forth. But this was something you saw all the time, and you took it and accepted it as a way of life. … And so there was no reason, in my estimation, when I left the scene, for any activity on May 1st."

As it turned out, Carson was wrong. Police cruisers patrolling the area were hit twice by beer bottles thrown by the students, but rather than respond, they simply pulled away and left the protesters to their own devices. Without anyone to stop them or even try to reason with them, the students escalated their behavior, including building a bonfire in the middle of the street and smashing the windows of nearby businesses (primarily banks and others that they saw as supporting the war effort).

The next day, Carson asked a friend what had gone wrong: "And I asked him what in the world had happened, because I'd been on the street an hour or two before that. And he said, well, things had gotten a little tense, and the police were not getting out of the cars, and they were not mixing with the crowd. And as they would zip by in the police cars the kids starting throwing rocks at these police cars. And, by that time, the guys had called the night sergeant, who was sitting down at city hall with his feet on his desk -- knowing him, I can say that--not wanting to respond. And not knowing what to do. The mayor and the safety director, who weren't really equipped for this kind of a situation, were out at the country club. It was May Day, and that used to be a place where you'd run out to dinner, maybe you played a little poker and had a few drinks, and by the time they were made aware of what was going on they were in no condition to be dealing with it. And so it got out of hand that night. And the mayor, rather than exercising reasonable judgment, called the sheriff in."

Indeed, Kent's mayor, Leroy Satrom, declared the city to be in a "state of emergency" and ordered the bars closed and the crowds dispersed. With that, the police began moving the students away from the downtown areas and back toward campus. By the end of the evening, police had arrested 14 students, most of them for refusing to move along.

Chapter 3: This Summer I hear the Drummin'

"One of our police officers was used to control the bar situation in a bar. He was actually an employee of the bar…to make sure everything was under control…And those people in the beginning who were throwing rocks were the motorcyclists, not the guys standing on their soap boxes preaching anarchy, because they weren't--even though there were a number of them, they weren't really taken that seriously…But that next morning, on the 2nd, we found out that the mayor then called a curfew for Saturday. The worst thing in the world." - John Carson

Following the incident on Friday night, many businessmen and city officials were concerned that the students would return and stage some sort of violent retaliation for being driven out of the area the night before. Thus, at the urging of both his advisors and his constituency, Satrom contacted Ohio Governor Jim Rhodes and asked that the state's Army National Guard be activated and sent to the town to keep order. Rhodes, a Republican who would go on to be one of the longest serving governors in American history, had a notoriously negative opinion of anti-war protesters, and he approved the use of the National Guard.

Governor Rhodes

By the time the National Guard arrived in Kent, it was 10:00 p.m. on the night of May 2nd, and more trouble was starting up. By that point, a large number of students had gathered in front of the Kent State ROTC building and had set it on fire. John Carson remembered, "But every kid in town knew it was going to be burned. My kids were there and they were early teenagers, because everybody was saying, go up and watch the burning. So the locals were up there in the crowd watching...And so that building was burned. It should have been torn down 20 years before that, so it really didn't matter...There were two ROTC buildings...but one was burned and then the other one was the ROTC building, but they were identical. They were just Quonset huts, wooden Quonset huts, kind of, for probably sleeping quarters, and they got converted into classrooms, and then ROTC. So even though they were burned it wouldn't have been a big deal had the university police responded properly. And they didn't get there."

Firefighters were unable to reach the blaze to put it out because of the hundreds of protesters crowded around the building, and many of the protesters turned violent, throwing objects at both the policemen and the firefighters. Some even stole hoses off the trucks and carried them to the nearby Commons, where they cut them to ribbons. Ellis Burns was a student on campus that night, and she subsequently described the scene: "I remember the fire department coming and unrolling the hoses and actually trying to put the fire out. And what really pissed me off was my peers, my [fellow] students, my [fellow] people protesting were actually cutting the fire hose, which made absolutely no sense to me. I just couldn't believe that that was happening, and I was a little bit disgusted about the whole thing. It was at that point, I think, that then the National Guard -- because there shortly after, the police and the National Guard, I don't remember all, who started to clear out and move people. Because, truly, if there was anybody in danger throughout this whole weekend, in my opinion, it might have been the firefighters…trying to put this fire out. That's the kind of thing that was really disturbing to me. The firemen were there. I was probably a little bit idealistic at the time. These guys didn't have anything to do with [anything] but put the fire out. I wasn't throwing rocks. Why are people throwing rocks? Why are they cutting the hoses? I understand the ROTC building what it represents. But it was just something that made no sense to me."

As Burns' account indicates, many of the students at Kent State were wholly uninvolved with protesting and had little if any interest in the protests. There's no question that plenty of them were also shocked by how far the protesters were going. Chuck Ayers recalled how he and his girlfriend learned of the incident while at his parents' house watching a baseball game: "We were sitting there watching the Indians game on TV, and they broke in with an announcement that, 'Rioting Kent State students had burned the ROTC building on campus.' … I heard this and I heard, 'Rampaging students have burned the ROTC building.' I thought, Oh God, what the hell? I'll go on campus and we'll see a little something. But Karen decided to call her roommates, and they said…from their room on the second floor they could see the flames from the building. They could already see…National Guard trucks on their street. There were helicopters flying over. I got on the phone with them, I could hear the helicopters over the telephone, and they said, 'Don't come back. You are not going to get back to the apartment tonight.' So she spent the night at my folks' house, and we got up early the next morning, Sunday morning, and drove up to campus."

One man who has remained anonymous through the years was both a student at Kent State and a member of the National Guard sent to quell the riots. As such, he had a rather unique perspective that night: "As we approached campus, which was evening…we had the top down on the jeep -- we had the top down on all the trucks. Canvas tops. You could see the fire, the glow of the fire on 76 as we approached Kent, and my first thought was, 'My God, the whole town is burning. The whole campus.' It was literally an orange glow in the sky…The tail of our group began setting up road blocks behind us as we went along. … As we approached campus, we met up with another group of the Guardsmen. ... Made a quick tour of town and campus. One of the groups was designated to go over, we understood, from the radio -- I understood from the radio traffic, that the building was on fire, that the firefighters were receiving some type of intervention from students; having difficulty doing their job. They were outnumbered. At that time a unit was sent over -- I was not in that unit. We patrolled parts of campus."

During the evening, the National Guard arrested many of the students and used tear gas to disperse the rest. Some of them even drew their bayonets in order to force the students to move. However, except for one person who received a small cut from a bayonet, no one was injured.

Chapter 4: Gotta Get Down to It

"I swear every few blocks there was a road block. And I just motioned everybody to go on through. I think it was at that time that I first realized what it meant to be in a military uniform in a civilian situation. Because we'd been out of the jeeps, we'd patrolled, it was evening, it was dark the night before of course, and things were pretty well settled down. And that was early in the morning. That was eight or nine o'clock in the morning -- Sunday morning. And one couple said, 'We're just simply goin' to church,' and all this. And it hit me then of the fact that here's a town that is now under siege and the military -- just like we've seen in the movies our whole life, of going into a civilian town and uh, it -- it just hit me...Funny that I stood there and reflect upon it thinking, 'My God, here's -- here I am, a 20-some-year-old kid with a gun, and people are pulling off to the streets for me.' We stayed there 'til about noon -- we were to leave -- we went back and got a meal at the school. We rested a little bit. And then we were put in the jeep to patrol the area." - Anonymous member of the Ohio National Guard

Many in Kent on Sunday morning, May 3, hoped that the violence would end once the students and everyone else had a chance to calm down, sober up, and consider the true gravity of their actions. In fact, that might very well have happened had local leaders tempered their reactions, but instead, Governor Rhodes gave a particularly provocative speech during the day: "We've seen here at the city of Kent especially, probably the most vicious form of campus oriented violence yet perpetrated by dissident groups. They make definite plans of burning, destroying, and throwing rocks at police, and at the National Guard and the Highway Patrol. This is when we're going to use every part of the law enforcement agency of Ohio to drive them out of Kent. We are going to eradicate the problem. We're not going to treat the symptoms. And these people just move from one campus to the other and terrorize the community. They're worse than the brown shirts and the communist element and also the night riders and the vigilantes. They're the worst type of people that we harbor in America. Now I want to say this. They are not going to take over campus. I think that we're up against the strongest, well-trained, militant, revolutionary group that has ever assembled in America."

Ironically, while Rhodes was fanning the flames with a speech that was clearly over the top, some students from Kent State had returned to the downtown area to begin cleaning up the mess they and their peers had made. It would have obviously been better if their actions gained more attention than Rhodes' speech, but not surprisingly, that was not even close to being the case. Instead, Governor Rhodes threatened to declare martial law, and Mayor Satrom declared a curfew in town.

In the meantime, Chuck Ayers and other students were simply trying to take in and process all that had happened. He described the tension in Kent the day before the shootings: "And as soon as we hit the city limits, there were army jeeps, there were trucks on the road, there were just about every large parking lot had at least one or two vehicles, either a truck or a couple of jeeps. They were going up and down the streets, there were army helicopters in the air, there were police helicopters in the air…there were jeeps and trucks everywhere, there were jeeps in the parking lot…and we were stopped by two Guardsmen. There was a roadblock across the street but we were on foot, so I thought we'd just walk up the sidewalk, and these guys yelled at us, 'Where the hell are you going?' I said, 'Going on campus.' 'You can't go through here.' And I said, 'Well, yeah, we can, we're students.' 'I don't care who you are, you can't walk here." And they were very angry, and with some reason.

At first, neither Ayers nor anyone else who had not been on campus the previous night could understand what all the fuss was about, but as he got closer to the ROTC building, he began to understand: "I could smell the burning building. That burnt-wood smell was all over, and that surprised me…And the smell kept getting stronger and stronger as we walked, and finally I topped that little bit of a hill and I could see it for the very first time, and I just stopped dead in my tracks because there was no building left. And I really did not expect that."

While it would be very easy to focus all of the attention on what the students went through during this chain of events, it's only fair to consider the fateful chain of events from the point of view of the National Guardsmen who had been called in at short notice to patrol a campus filled with students. Ayers himself noted, "One of the guys I worked with…was in the National Guard at the time. He had been on campus that day. I didn't know it at the time, but he had been called up a few days earlier for that Teamster strike; and …there was shooting at these truck convoys that were being escorted by National Guard from overpasses. So these guys had already been in a very awful situation. They were probably fearing for their lives working on the Teamster strike, and then they're pulled away from that and they're on a college campus where they're the same age as everybody that's there, but they're the guys in the uniforms with the guns and it's their job to yell at people, keep them from going here and going there."

At the same time, while a lot of students were ardently protesting and some were violent, other students were simply perplexed by everything. Likewise, members of the community who had lived near each other for decades found themselves at odds, and for at least one member of the

National Guard, the situation was positively surreal: "And all we were doing was show-of-force type of thing. We were just driving through the streets…And we stopped at a stop sign and some kids came out on their porch and started throwing stuff at us -- bottles and stuff like that, and, and uh, a jeep pulled up behind us and I recall the one fella getting out and taking out his rifle and just pointing and said, 'Who wants to be first?' And they all dispersed and went back into the crowd. … And another jeep came and we stopped and we were talking, and another vehicle -- there were six or eight of us -- and I recall this very nice, grey-haired lady coming out of her house with a plateful of cookies, and saying, 'Here guys,' ya know, 'here's some homemade cookies for you.' So you went a matter of a hundred feet from one contrast of someone throwing something at you and calling you names and obscenities and giving you the finger, to an older lady coming out and offering you cookies -- ya know, from her home and town."

Though Sunday mostly remained quiet until nightfall, the evening brought more trouble. A group of students gathered on the Commons at 8:00 p.m., one of whom was Carol Mirman, a 21 year old student caught up in the excitement. She recalled, "And as it became darker word was going through the crowd…that we needed to disperse, and after a certain hour we were to stay on campus and were no longer allowed to leave campus. I was exceedingly irate about that. 'What is this war -- its war here.' I mean this is ridiculous. Nobody's really done anything. I didn't support the ROTC Building being burned down but nonetheless that didn't mean the tanks had to come. That didn't mean that Guards and people with guns and bayonets and teargas and helicopters had to come. But, sure enough, there they all were. And as night approached and the helicopters there thup-thup-thupping overhead and the strobe lights were flashing which was a sense of complete unreality -- I was thinking 'Phooey with those guys. Who says we can't go someplace. This is my school, my campus, and my country. This is America, ya know. I have rights -- 21-year-old rights (I was 21 years old) -- and I want to go where I want to go.'"

In keeping with their orders, the Guardsmen began marching toward the students and ordering them to disperse, but far from being hardened veterans, these were young men, some of whom had been students sitting in class on the Kent State campus days earlier. As a result, many of those in uniform were as frightened and unsure of themselves as those with the rocks.

One of the Guardsmen remembered, "And they started moving and shouting, 'Here we come!' And they did. …and I thought, 'What are we gonna do now?' And a lot of thoughts ran through my mind. If we're told to lock and load are we going to fire, are we gonna protect our lives, are we going to run? A lot of things go through your mind. Not only as a civilian but as a soldier…You know you have two types of training. You have civilian training and you very quickly -- soldier training. One of the worst things you can do as a soldier is retreat. But then again, we were National Guard. So a lot of things go through your mind. A lot of the men that were in with me were my contemporaries, if you will, in age, in background -- a lot of rubber workers, some college students. No one of any significance or importance, just a group of men that were there for a common reason."

According to one member of the National Guard, the guns they were carrying were never loaded that Sunday night: "And the captain came along and said to us … that, … When the order is given to lock and load … That you are to lock and load, but you are NOT" -- and he made it very clear, 'Do NOT under any circumstances fire unless you are given the order. And do not lock and load until you are told to lock and load.' I don't believe that evening we had locked and loaded." Instead, the soldiers relied on the force of their presence to intimidate the students into moving, but at that point, another confrontation occurred, one that escalated the situation. The Guardsman reported, "A group came up holding a white flag -- three or four individuals holding a white flag -- and they said they wanted to talk to us. One individual was holding a white flag and there were two or three males with him, and the captain says, 'Easy, easy, don't do anything. Maybe we can calm this crowd down.' Maybe they were leaders -- they were waving a white flag -- and they got about 25 feet away from us and they unloaded with a barrage of rocks. So, it wasn't a sign of 'let's talk.' And the three out of the four men just delved into their pockets and started throwing rocks. The one officer at that point let a 79 grenade go, and hit a guy right in the shoulder with it. I know to this day, that guy's shoulder isn't right. It's then that I saw what we were dealing with…We then dispersed that crowd with tear gas. We just got the order to lay down tear gas."

After the use of teargas, the students left that area, but then they reassembled nearby at the corner of Lincoln and Main in Kent. From there, the students staged an impromptu sit-in until about 11:00 p.m., when the National Guard again approached them and ordered them to return to their homes in accordance with the terms of the curfew. As they were nudging the students away from the corner, a few suffered minor cuts from contact with a bayonet. The Guardsman remembered:

"[W]e were actually told that we were going to stop the crowd from going downtown ...Which I knew some of the businessmen in town, and I -- believe me, to this day I think it's just as well because, believe me, they were better armed than we were, and had those students goin' downtown…and had those people moved on downtown to trash it again, there would have been gunfire…It's at that point that I saw the students again let go with the rocks--and men standing there waving their genitals at us, and women shouting obscenities...and I was no virgin, and I was used to a lot of things, but not on my campus. And I looked at this and I said, 'This gives me a whole different point of view on what's happening here again.'

We then were separated...we were to hold our ground. They were coming up…shouting, yelling, throwing things at us. We're still moving up -- toward downtown on campus…The crowd behind us seemed somewhat to disperse. We laid some gas back there…we had helicopters in the sky -- a lot of radio traffic, a lot of bullhorns…We did what they call a stutter step…where you put your rifle down at your side and you step up…I think at that point in time that got a lot of people's attention because they saw that we weren't going to be intimidated, and we moved.

It's safe to assume that many people in Kent wondered why the students continued to march against the National Guard. After all, they were outgunned, no one had yet been hurt, and there were no television cameras around. In the eyes of the Guardsman, the students were being led by outsiders: "It's at this point in time that I very quickly became aware of what was happening on Kent State University campus. I had been on this campus for four years -- there were a lot of people. I noted very quickly that the people as they approached the crowd were older people -- older men and women, a lot of which I had never seen on campus. They brought the crowd to us -- small groups, 50, 60, 80, 100 people -- they would bring the crowds to us. I know the faces. If I see them today, I would know their faces. Quickly they were in front of the crowd, they quickly dispersed, went around behind the crowd, locked hands -- this was a group of ten or fifteen people -- and pushed the crowd into us. So what were the leaders, dispersed and went behind the group and pushed them into us. This is the point where we got hit with rocks, human feces in plastic bags -- uh, we were given the finger, we were yelled at. Things came flying out of the air, it was weird. It was dark, but the light -- a lot of lights -- but things were flying out of the air."

Chapter 5: Should Have Been Done Long Ago

"We were walking around pretty much without our gear on, and the old 'Get it on' came and we went over and got our weapons -- fell in -- got in formation, and we marched up out of the stadium and marched up to -- again -- to the ROTC area, and they said, 'There's some -- kids are forming again,' and we said, 'Oh, not this shit again.' You know, we'd been through this, we're tired, why don't these kids go to school where they belong? And a lot of us started thinking, 'Why aren't they in class? "What's goin' on with these people?' You know, why aren't they there? Yeah, ya know, let's get on with our lives here, and let's get back -- the fun's over -- the night before, we had a couple days, and they burned a building and -- we really were under the impression, and everyone was, that now that school's starting, it's back to the college kid-type thing. It wasn't that way." - Ohio National Guardsman

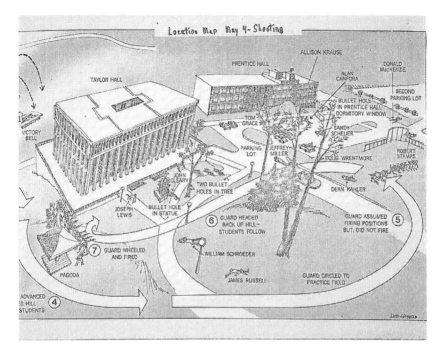

A map showing the marching route of the National Guard on May 4

The fateful gathering of the protesting students began at noon on Monday, May 4, despite the fact that by this time, the university's leadership had officially banned the event and passed out more than 12,000 flyers warning students that the event had been cancelled. Undeterred, at least 2,000 people ignored those leaflets and gathered on the Commons anyway, including Ellis Burns. Burns explained, "I got to the Victory Bell, and there were a bunch of people there. We were there to make a stand, and I was there to make a stand. So what happened was I was just hanging around, and again I felt strongly about why I was there. I kind of felt like I had a purpose. I really wanted [the National Guard] to be off. And then the whole thing kind of started. That's when they came out with the bullhorns and the jeep and they said, 'You will disperse. You're in violation of some state emergency ordinance or emergency martial law, and if you don't disperse within a period of time, people are going to be arrested,' or whatever they said. We were all just like, no, we're not moving, this is just what we're gonna do.

By this time, the National Guard units were also present and in place, but they numbered just under 80 men, and when the Guardsmen ordered the students to leave, they were met with increasingly hostile refusals. At one point late in the morning, Harold Rice, a member of the campus police department, rode in a National Guard jeep up to the group of protesters and again ordered them to leave, but the protesters threw rocks at both Rice and his driver until they pulled away. Rice subsequently returned just before the protest was to start and again ordered the students to disperse. One Guardsman remembered, "We got down on campus -- hastily again -- brought back over to the campus where we were around the ROTC building -- formed up in a line. There was a company from Ravenna, I believe, and our company, 'C' company. In fact there was a map I saw in the paper the other day that showed where 'C' company was. And the 'C' company was to go up around the other side of Taylor -- to the left, if you will -- Taylor Hall. But again, you have to realize the mish-mash we were in. We were lined up, sometimes double, and the group I was in, and some of my men, ended up going up to the right. ... Oh, they tried. They didn't do it by division as much as saying, 'A platoon or third platoon,' it was 'From here over, you go that way; from here over you follow that way.' ... We were put in formation -- Single line, and then we form a double line and that kind of stuff."

When the students again refused, the National Guard lobbed teargas into the crowds, but it was a windy day that rendered the teargas less effective. Instead, it only provoked the students into throwing more rocks at the Guardsmen, and the protesters began to taunt the Guardsmen with a chant of "Pigs off campus!"

When the tear gas failed to disperse the crowds, the Guardsmen were ordered by their superiors to fix the bayonets to the end of their rifles and advance on the crowd. Seeing the soldiers approaching, the protesters scurried away over nearby Blanket Hill. Burns explained, "Then you started to see the advance of all the Guardsmen. They started to advance. Here we are, it was Blanket Hill, and we were standing there. It's kind of like, these guys got guns, and they're coming toward us. And you don't know, you don't think about what's going to happen, you don't know exactly what's going to happen. But as they moved towards us and they got closer and closer, I believe it was then that they started firing tear gas. So we all started running away from the tear gas, because I remember I had Kleenex and so on, and I remember rubbing my eyes and all the appropriate things you were supposed to do at that time to try and minimize the amount of damage that the tear gas did."

Once over the hill, the students split into different groups, with one body of protesters moving along toward nearby Taylor Hall and the other toward Prentice Hall. The soldiers followed the protesters over the hill, but instead of following the students, the Guardsmen continued in a straight line towards an athletic field. Unfortunately, the field was surrounded on most sides by a chain link fence, so the men could not figure out how to get out of it. From Burns' perspective, it was then the students who had the upper hand: "I think it was the National Guard was coming up over the hill and eventually ended up over on the old practice field. People were dispersing, running around. It was thick with tear gas. I was kind of at the top where Taylor Hall was, looking down. The great picture where it shows the students looking down. The National Guard was basically, if there was a time for them that they were in danger it was probably that time, because they truly were surrounded. Because they had a fence on one side and there were students on the other two or three sides around them. I remember they kind of stopped, almost like they were resting. They kind of stopped, because they didn't know what the next action would be. It was at that point then that they started to lob some tear gas, and I remember seeing some of the protesters -- some of my colleagues, if you will -- some of the protesters starting to throw the tear gas back. And then another National Guard picked up some tear gas canister, threw it back. Then another person threw it back. And at that point they started to march back up the hill, up towards the Pagoda."

Seemingly pinned down in this position, the soldiers were face to face with the students, most of whom were in front of Taylor Hall. Some began to leave and were making their way across the parking lot between Taylor Hall and Prentice Hall, and it was during this time, while they were facing the parking lot, that the guardsmen took an offensive position by kneeling down and aiming their guns at the parking lot. However, after a moment in this position, they were ordered to stand up again.

With the standoff in process, groups of soldiers were meeting in one place while groups of students met about a dozen yards away. It seemed that everyone was trying to decide what to do next. After a few minutes passed, the Guardsmen began moving back up the hill, returning the way they had come, but as they did so, students followed them. One Guardsman summarized the movements: "Again, there was a group maybe a hundred yards in front of the small group I was in. We came up behind a group. A group went down over what was the soccer field or some practice field. I remember the group over by the dorm, they were left at Taylor Hall, and then we retreated."

Many people, like Chuck Ayers, thought the confrontation was over at that point. He explained, "So anyway, I watched this for a while, and the guys that were kneeling finally stood up and sort of rejoined the line. And they sort of did, not an about-face, but they were walking down, training down the line that they had been standing in, walking towards the end of the football field...And I remember thinking, I haven't seen any tear gas for a while, they must have run out of tear gas, so I think it's over. So they marched down the line that way, then all of a sudden they just, the whole line did a right-face, and they started marching across, from side to side, on the practice football field...I was aware that, as the Guard moved...that it was going to put me again right between the two groups...I turned, I walked in the door of Taylor Hall...And I never even heard the shots."

Chapter 6: Soldiers Are Gunning Us Down

"My boyfriend said to me, 'I think that's bullets.' And I panicked. I turned around and I decided that I was going to run across the parking lot in the same direction from where I had just come, in the same path that I had followed, right along the cars, because there was a little dip in the land there where you can roll down a hill. In my mind - everybody was getting down - but I decided to run and that I was going to run there and roll down the hill and that I'd be safe. It's just, you know, I wasn't thinking. And my boyfriend was running after me, screaming, 'Get down! Get down!'…He just hit me in mid-air and knocked me down and threw himself on top of me. And at that point the shooting stopped. We stayed there for a few seconds…I thought maybe he had been shot, because we didn't move, and then we stood up and I kept running. I just was determined I was going to get - I didn't know if they were going to shoot again or what, and I just kept running, and he said, 'Where are you going? Don't run.' And I - nobody could've stopped me." - Catherine Delattre

At 12:24 p.m., less than an hour after the students began gathering, the worst case scenario played itself out. As the National Guard was marching back in the direction from which they had originally come, protesters continued to hurl rocks at them from a distance, and while it's unclear what prompted the shooting, it was around that time that eyewitnesses claimed Sergeant Myron Pryor turned back in the direction of the students and began firing his sidearm, a .45 pistol. Hearing that shot, the soldiers standing nearest him assumed an order had been given and also opened fire. Over at least the next 13 seconds, 29 of the Guardsmen fired 67 rounds; some of the shots were aimed intentionally high or into the ground, but others hit the crowd. One eyewitness claimed, "The shots were definitely coming my way, because when a bullet passes your head, it makes a crack. I hit the ground behind the curve, looking over. I saw a student hit. He stumbled and fell, to where he was running towards the car. Another student tried to pull him behind the car, bullets were coming through the windows of the car. As this student fell behind the car, I saw another student go down, next to the curb, on the far side of the automobile, maybe 25 or 30 yards from where I was lying. It was maybe 25, 30, 35 seconds of sporadic firing. The firing stopped. I lay there maybe 10 or 15 seconds. I got up, I saw four or five students lying around the lot. By this time, it was like mass hysteria. Students were crying, they were screaming for ambulances. I heard some girl screaming, 'They didn't have blank, they didn't have blank,' no, they didn't." Similarly, John Kifner, a reporter for *The New York Times*, wrote, "The crackle of the rifle volley cut the suddenly still air. It appeared to go on, as a solid volley, for perhaps a full minute or a little longer. Some of the students dived to the ground, crawling on the grass in terror. Others stood shocked or half crouched, apparently believing the troops were firing into the air. Some of the rifle barrels were pointed upward."

To this day, no one has definitively figured out why the Guardsmen opened fire, but plenty of protesters thought it was ordered. Dr. Jerry Lewis, a professor on the campus that day, noted the manner in which the Guardsmen wheeled in unison and fired: "Obviously, if you turn together in close quarters with bayonet, there must be some coordination, but I've always interpreted as that they planned to fire but fire high — because they were angry ... they were poorly led ... their tear gas masks didn't work properly. But many people have used the turning together — and there were lots of eyewitnesses to that — as [a sign] that there was a rough agreement to do that, or that there was an order. But I haven't seen any evidence yet that there was an order."

In this picture of the vantage point of the National Guardsmen when they opened fire, Taylor Hall is on the left, Prentice Hall is in the background, and the parking lot is in the center.

Frederick P. Wenger, the Assistant Adjutant General of the Ohio National Guard, argued that a sniper had fired on the National Guard and compelled the Guardsmen to respond with live rounds: "They were understanding orders to take cover and return any fire." Whether there was actually a sniper remains unclear, but in the confusion that followed, no sniper was ever found or identified. Kifner, the reporter for *The New York Times*, wrote, "This reporter, who was with the group of students, did not see any indication of sniper fire, nor was the sound of any gunfire audible before the Guard volley. Students, conceding that rocks had been thrown, heatedly denied that there was any sniper."

At the time of the shooting, most of the students were at least 150 feet away from the Guardsmen, but for those who lay bleeding on the ground that day, it didn't much matter why the National Guard had opened fire. One of the most severely wounded was Dean Kahler, who had been shot in the spine and was permanently paralyzed. In an interview years later, Kahler shared one of his first memories in the hospital: "The first card that I opened up in the intensive care unit was a very nice-looking card, but the note in it said, 'Dear communist hippie radical, I hope by the time you read this, you are dead.'"

Ellen Mann later related a story about another one young man who was badly injured: "Then Joseph Lewis was standing about four or five feet from me…I stood there and I watched as the Guard, they were already down the hill when I got up there. They had turned and they were in the – there's a big parking lot down there and they were all clustered together. Some of them were talking, some of them were messing with their guns, and a couple of them were bent down and pointing guns, like, aiming at people. At that point I thought, 'Hmm, well those guns don't have bullets. They wouldn't have live ammunition in a campus unrest.' I just didn't think of it. As I watched, they came back up the hill, and they came to the Pagoda, and they were all marching together. And they suddenly turned. They turned all at the same time, and they went like this. At that point I looked at Joseph, and I saw he was giving them the finger. The next thing I know, he falls, he screams, 'Oh my God, they shot me!' And he falls to the ground. I mean, he was -- maybe from me to the wall there -- probably about four feet, five feet. And I rushed right over to him. He was kind of wriggling around. He was in pain. A couple of other guys came up, and we took his pants down -- he was laying on his right side -- we took his pants down, because there was a lot of blood. So we unzipped his jeans, pulled it down, and there was a hole blown out of him. It was really gory and really bloody."

In addition to Kahler and Lewis, John Cleary was also shot. He was much closer to the Guardsmen than the other students and had been hit in the upper chest on the left side. Thomas Grace and Alan Canfora suffered only minor injuries after being hit in the left ankle and the right wrist respectively, while Doug Wrentmore was shot in his right knee and James Russell received to two minor wounds, one to his thigh and one across his forehead. Bobby Stamps received a minor but embarrassing injury, as Catherine Delattre explained: "And I just ran and I got to the end of that, and I remember I got down and I rolled down the hill. And there was somebody - I think it was Bobby Stamps that had been shot in the buttock - was there and we walked over to the building, and he went in there was waiting for help. Just you know, very unreal. And I walked in there, and I saw him, and he had pulled his pants down because he just had a hole in his backside. Then we walked out of that and started back through the parking lot and saw each person who had been killed. It was just horrendous." The final shooting victim to survive was Donald MacKenzie, who suffered a minor neck wound.

Alan Canfora at the annual May 4 Commemoration at Kent State in 2008

In the meantime, most of the members of the National Guard were as confused about what had happened as the students were. There had seemingly been no orders to shoot, nor a plan for this kind of outcome, and far less than half of the Guardsmen had even opened fire. As a result, the Guardsmen had to react on instinct rather than with a plan. Ronald Snyder, one of the officers, explained, "[A]round 12:20, we heard gunfire. We seen a number of students running to--which at the time we didn't know where they were running to…. And then we--in fact we--there was kind of like a--if I remember right, it was kind of like a triangle out in front of us, and we were standing between the two halls, the company, and the gunfire occurred…Because the way the two halls was, it initially sounded like it was coming from the left, but it turned out it was coming from the right, probably because of the acoustics of the one building. If I remember right, I believe some stone was flying from the one building that got hit by some rounds. Anyway, we see immediately that some students were hit. As I recall, I called for the ambulances at that time, because we had what we called a command post, I think it was down in front of the library or thereabouts, and we asked that they send the ambulances up. And then I kind of moved forward with a small squad or a couple men. In fact, if you look at the pictures, there was that young lady from Florida that was kneeling over one of the bodies."

That young lady was Mary Ann Vecheio, a 14 year old runaway who was on campus that day to protest the war. The photo of her kneeling over a dead body would become the most poignant symbol of everything that happened at Kent State that day.

Chapter 7: Four Dead in Ohio

"After the guns started shooting, it was deathly quiet for a long time. It seemed like forever. But it was probably not that long, because then people started screaming and wailing and hollering. Then pandemonium broke out. I saw Joseph, and I saw the guy by that sculpture, but I didn't see anybody else because I just, I just couldn't believe what had happened. So the ambulances finally got there, and I walked to the ambulance with them, and watched them put him into the ambulance." - Ellen Mann

While it was tragic enough that a handful of protesters had been injured, four young students paid the ultimate price, and two of them had not even taken part in the protests. Ellis Burns had made it through unscathed, but he immediately realized how lucky he had been:

> "So [Sandy Scheuer and I] were walking away and we were over in the parking lot, and that's when we heard the -- and I'll say the firing, but we didn't know what it was. I can say I didn't know what it was. All I knew was, instinctually, what I knew was this wasn't right. In a split second, I knew that I was going to grab her and we were going to go to some type of cover. And that's all I knew. I don't know why. Never fired a gun, never fired once. But I heard a volley of shots that I don't think I'll ever forget. It just seemed to last forever. We both hit the ground. I had my arm around her, my left arm around her. We both were kind of diving, if you will, towards cover. Not sure why, other than we just knew we didn't want to be standing. We dove for cover, and I remember waiting until I felt it was safe to get up. Until we felt like the shooting was over. You didn't know it was shooting. It felt like it was shooting. You knew it was some kind of shooting. So you waited, and I couldn't even begin to tell you how long we waited for. But we waited. Finally, you can kind of hear things in the background, kind of indicating that you're -- you hear people screaming, and then you realize, okay.
>
> I remember I had my arm around her, and she was laying on her stomach face down. I remember calling out to her, 'Sandy, it's over. Let's go, let's go.' I

remember calling out to her, and there was no response. And then I looked. And then I realized that I believe she had been, she was hit, I think it was the left side or the right side? I think it was the right side. I could be a little off on this. It had to be the right side. The right side, because the bullet had not just grazed her but had severed a carotid artery. So there was a lot of blood. I was in a state of like, I don't know what to do. I remember trying to administer first aid. I remember trying to reach in, to try to stop the bleeding into her neck, because you could just see where the bullet had penetrated her carotid artery. I think it was her carotid artery, I'm not a doctor. But there was just blood all over. And she was totally unconscious.

I remember calling out for help, calling an ambulance, which seemed like an eternity. People came over to try to help out. We moved her. We tried to revive her. We tried some CPR. We just wanted to stop the bleeding. I remember trying to lift her feet so we could keep blood going to her brain. But it seemed totally unsuccessful. And then finally an ambulance arrived. I remember asking somebody in the ambulance, 'I want to go with her.' And they said, 'No, absolutely not.' So that was it. There are some accounts, I believe I have heard that she actually had a heartbeat to the hospital, but I can't attest to that at all. In my mind, she had died right there. Because to the best of my knowledge, she had never gained consciousness again. We did everything we could, but it was just a complete, it was just a really, you just couldn't believe it."

Sandy, a 20 year old student at Kent State, had been hit in the neck despite being nearly 400 feet away from the Guardsmen and died of blood loss within minutes. She was not participating in the protest; as Ellis Burns' account makes painfully clear, she was simply in the wrong place at the wrong time.

Also killed that day was Allison Krause, a 19 year old who had suffered a fatal chest wound. Unlike Scheuer, Krause was involved in the protest, but she was nearly 350 feet away from the Guardsmen who opened fire. She was later eulogized by Barry Levine, her boyfriend at the time, who quoted her as saying, "Flowers are better than bullets."

As Krause lay bleeding to death, Jeff Miller lay lifeless where he had fallen, killed instantly by a shot through his mouth. Like many 20 years old, Miller avidly opposed the Vietnam War, and he had avoided the 1969 draft lottery with a deferment thanks to his status as a student at Kent State. It was Miller's body that Mary Ann Vecchio was kneeling over in John Filo's famous photograph, which went on to win the Pulitzer Prize. Chuck Ayers later described the scene: "I went back up the same stairwell I'd come out, I came back out the same door, and the very first thing I saw was Jeff Miller in the street. Initially, I found out when he fell he was face-down, chest-down, his head to the side, and somebody had turned him over, and there were several people kneeling around him, and there was already this river of blood rolling down, I mean it must have been 12 to 15 feet long at that time…I was 22. And there was this guy in the street, and I kept saying to myself, No, he's not dead, they'll patch him up, he'll be okay. And I just remember looking at how utterly limp he was--and they had pulled his shirt up--and how absolutely hollow his stomach looked. Everything had just collapsed on this guy. And I kept saying to myself, No he's not dead, he's not dead, until I heard an ambulance come up over the hill and started picking up people, and the gurneys went right past him. Oh my God, he's dead, because they didn't stop to pick him up."

John Filo at the annual May 4 Commemoration at Kent State in 2008

Filo and Mary Ann Vecchio at the annual May 4 Commemoration at Kent State in 2008

A memorial at the spot where Miller was killed

The final fatality that day was the most ironic of all. William Schroeder was a native of Ohio and the quintessential All-American boy who had graduated with honors from high school. He was also an Eagle Scout and a recipient of the Association of the United States Army Award for Excellence in History. He was a member of the Kent State ROTC and was in no way involved in the protests against the war or anything else. Like Sandy Scheuer, he was simply trying to get to class, and at the time he was shot, he was lying face down on the ground and facing away from the Guardsmen. As his college roommate put it, "Bill was 332 feet away from the nearest National Guardsman, not much of a threat. He was shot with a folder in his hand." Having been shot in the chest, Schroeder survived long enough to reach a nearby hospital but died shortly thereafter during surgery.

Chapter 8: How Can You Run When You Know?

"So May 4th was a very upsetting thing for us as a family, but mostly on a personal level. My brother Mark had been killed in Vietnam in '69, and my mom had been against the war, and my father had been for the war, and suddenly, the whole war just didn't matter anymore, with Dad dying, and Mom at his side…And she said, 'He's gone.'…She says, 'You just won't believe,' she says, 'I was upstairs, and the -- all of a sudden there was all this noise and commotion. And then all these young people were wheeled into the ICU, from the shootings. And the doctors and the nurses were just crying. And one doctor went over and he held an x-ray up, and he was holding it, showing it to another doctor. And he said, "Look where this bullet is lodged. This bullet is lodged in this boy's spine. He's never going to walk again. In all my years of medicine, this is the most senseless thing I've ever seen."' So my mom said, 'Lord, Nick has had 55 good years. All this time, all this month, I've been praying that you would spare him. But how can I ask for that when these kids haven't even had twenty years? From now on, it's whatever you want.' She turned around and went back into the ICU, and he had died." - Timothy DeFrange.

In the moments immediately following the shooting, most people outdoors were in a panic, looking only for a way to escape the area. However, there were a few men who were in charge to the campus that day who felt responsible for trying to prevent any more deaths or injuries. Dr. Jerry Lewis later related his reaction to seeing the students down: "So I stood up, and I remember saying to myself, 'What should I do?' And I describe this in other places as having a lifeguard mentality, which I was. I realized my first responsibility was to the students, but I didn't know what to do. And a student who knew me rushed up, and said, 'Dr. Lewis, those were blanks, weren't they?' Now I realized that the students all thought that they were firing blanks. So I pointed -- I didn't know it was Sandy Scheuer's body, but I pointed at the body…and said, 'No, those were real bullets.' And I realized the students had to get out of there. So I began to running around to the back of the Prentice Hall parking lot saying, 'Those are real bullets. You must leave. I'm Dr. Lewis. You must leave.' And I think people did leave. Then an RA (Residential Assistant) came to me, and said, 'Dr. Lewis, go on the microphone in Prentice Hall,' which I did. So I broadcasted to all of Prentice Hall that they were real bullets. But I think people had begun to figure that out."

Lewis was joined in his appeal by Glenn Frank, another member of the faculty who stepped up to address the students. Frank pleaded passionately, "I don't care whether you've never listened to anyone before in your lives. I am begging you right now. If you don't disperse right now, they're going to move in, and it can only be a slaughter. Would you please listen to me? Jesus Christ, I don't want to be a part of this!" Frank's son would later praise his father's quick thinking and assert, "He absolutely saved my life and hundreds of others".

As the students dispersed and the ambulances hauled away the injured, meetings began around the country to decide what to do next. On the most local level, the president of Kent State decided to close down the campus for six weeks to allow everyone involved in the tragedy to catch their breath. Likewise, the students present that day took time to consider what had happened and the real price they were paying for their beliefs. While some decided to continue their activism, most began to slowly distance themselves from the war and politics. On the other hand, others who had previously been more ambivalent joined the movement out of a sense of outrage at what had happened.

One of the positive things that came out of the Kent State shootings was the realization on people's part that violence led to more violence. Timothy Moore was among those who helped work toward finding peaceful ways for getting everyone's voices heard. He explained, "[I]n 1971 I became President of Black United Students. Part of my platform was the recognition that many black students were being alienated from BUS because they weren't interested in violence. They weren't interested in a revolution that had a violent dimension to it. There was a big concern because certain people felt--they were preoccupied with what we called the 'blacker than thou' mentality: that if you didn't subscribe to the same tenants of being black that they felt you should, then you were not 'down with them,' so to speak. So certain people started feeling alienated from the Black United Students because of this kind of revolutionary rhetoric."

At the state and local level, the decision was made to leave the National Guard in place for a time, even as all those who had fired their weapons that day were brought in for interrogation. Over the next several years, there would be a plethora of hearings, criminal cases, and civil cases, and while conspiracy theories continue to be prevalent, nobody has been able to prove anything definitive beyond the fact that it was a terrible tragedy. That said, President's Commission on Campus Unrest concluded in September 1970, "Even if the guardsmen faced danger, it was not a danger that called for lethal force. The 61 shots by 28 guardsmen certainly cannot be justified. Apparently, no order to fire was given, and there was inadequate fire control discipline on Blanket Hill. The Kent State tragedy must mark the last time that, as a matter of course, loaded rifles are issued to guardsmen confronting student demonstrators." In another section of the report, the language was even more forceful: "[T]he indiscriminate firing of rifles into a crowd of students and the deaths that followed were unnecessary, unwarranted, and inexcusable."

This same sense of caution was felt by those in the federal government. While many older politicians had disparaged anti-war protesters before, many in government were filled with a sense of shock and horror at how far things had gotten out of hand. Even still, President Nixon's statement had a hint of blaming the victims in it: "This should remind us all once again that when dissent turns to violence it invites tragedy. It is my hope that this tragic and unfortunate incident will strengthen the determination of all the nation's campuses, administrators, faculty and students alike to stand firmly for the right which exists in this country of peaceful dissent and just as strong against the resort to violence as a means of such expression." Nixon would subsequently attempt to conduct secret surveillance of anti-war group leaders, a plan that was resisted by FBI Director J. Edgar Hoover.

Investigations were ordered to make sure that something like the Kent State shootings could never happen again, and task forces were put together to determine better, less dangerous ways to quell rioters. Of course, there were all kinds of civil suits as the families of victims sought not just justice but answers. One suit charged everyone from the Guardsmen to the president of Kent State and Governor Rhodes with wrongful death, and when the Sixth Circuit Court of Appeals reversed judgments in the defendants' favor, the case was settled out of court. As part of that settlement, the defendants issued a statement of regret:

> "In retrospect, the tragedy of May 4, 1970 should not have occurred. The students may have believed that they were right in continuing their mass protest in response to the Cambodian invasion, even though this protest followed the posting and reading by the university of an order to ban rallies and an order to disperse. These orders have since been determined by the Sixth Circuit Court of Appeals to have been lawful.
>
> Some of the Guardsmen on Blanket Hill, fearful and anxious from prior events, may have believed in their own minds that their lives were in danger. Hindsight suggests that another method would have resolved the confrontation. Better ways must be found to deal with such a confrontation.
>
> We devoutly wish that a means had been found to avoid the May 4th events culminating in the Guard shootings and the irreversible deaths and injuries. We deeply regret those events and are profoundly saddened by the deaths of four students and the wounding of nine others which resulted. We hope that the agreement to end the litigation will help to assuage the tragic memories regarding that sad day."

In a way, the shootings at Kent State marked both the high point and low point of the anti-war movement; never again would students feel freedom to throw rocks and protest in non-peaceful ways, but at the same time, the government could never assume that sending in young men with guns to quell such riots was appropriate, let alone wise. To this day, whenever there are accusations that law enforcement authorities have cracked down on protests in an overly aggressive manner, the reverberations of Kent State are keenly felt.

Bibliography

Agte, Barbara Becker, (2012), *Kent Letters: Students' Responses to the May 1970 Massacre.* Deming, New Mexico: Bluewaters Press.

Bills, Scott. (1988). *Kent State/May 4: Echoes Through a Decade.* Kent, Ohio: Kent State University Press.

Caputo, Philip. (2005). *13 Seconds: A Look Back at the Kent State Shootings* with DVD. New York: Chamberlain Bros.

Davies, Peter and the Board of Church and Society of the United Methodist Church.

(1973). *The Truth About Kent State: A Challenge to the American Conscience.* New York: Farrar, Straus & Giroux.

Eszterhas, Joe, and Michael D. Roberts (1970). *Thirteen Seconds: Confrontation at Kent State.* New York: Dodd, Mead.

Gordon, William A. (1990). *The Fourth of May: Killings and Coverups at Kent State.* Buffalo, New York: Prometheus Books.

Michener, James. (1971). *Kent State: What Happened and Why.* New York: Random House and Reader's Digest Books.

Payne, J. Gregory (1981). *Mayday: Kent State*. Dubuque, Iowa: Kendall/Hunt Pub. Co.

Report of the President's Commission on Campus Unrest ("Scranton Commission"). (1970) Washington, D.C.: U.S. Government Printing Office.

Made in the USA
Middletown, DE
28 July 2017